Bird City, American Eye

ALSO BY
AHREND TORREY

Small Blue Harbor

Bird City, American Eye

POEMS & PROEMS BY

AHREND TORREY

PINYON PUBLISHING
Montrose, Colorado

Cover Art "Couple of Ibis Birds Nesting" by beastfromeast

Photographs of Ahrend Torrey by Jonathan Dacula
Lafreniere Park in Metairie, Louisiana, February 23, 2022

First Edition: April 2022

Pinyon Publishing
23847 V66 Trail, Montrose, CO 81403
www.pinyon-publishing.com

Library of Congress Control Number: 2022933806
ISBN: 978-1-936671-81-6

ACKNOWLEDGMENTS

I wish to thank the editors of the journals where some of these poems were first published, though sometimes in earlier versions and with slightly different titles:

Amethyst Magazine: "A Question About African Violets"; "On Becoming the Waves"

Cosumnes River Journal: "Yesterday I Cut the Grass"

Clear Poetry: "You Know"

Curator Magazine: "During Saga Dawa, I Walk to the Marsh; You Should Too"; "This Moment is Blue Jay"

Etruscan Press: "Cascade" selected as the Etruscan Prize winner

Eunoia Review: "Rising Light"

Foxglove Journal: "Drifting"

Havik Anthology: "At Audubon Park, A Lady Asked"; "Daffodils"

Metafore Magazine: "For What Are the Blossoms Reaching"; "Just as You Are"; "Semifaith"

Molecule LitMag: "Louisiana Irises, Basking in the Sun"

Moria: "Li Po," nominated for the 2019 Best New Poets Anthology

Muddy River Poetry Review: "I Lie in Bed Late at Night in New Orleans"

Peculiar Journal: "Like a Ghost-bird at Night"

Plum Tree Tavern: "On Visiting an Unnamed Swamp"

Proem: "Three Stories About Strangers" nominated for the 2021 Pushcart Prize

Red Eft Review: "The Ant"

Seven Circle Press: "On Being Human"

Stormy Island Publishing: "~~A Sand Poem I Wrote~~"; "I See the School Board Rush into the Café"; "Some Say the City is Louder"

The Dawntreader: "When Death Comes"

The Edge Magazine: "Crossing Lake Pontchartrain, I Drive Through a Swarm of Blind Mosquitos"; "Somewhere, Duck"

The Tiger Moth Review: "At a Streetcar Stop"

Third Wednesday: "Mary"

Tiny Seed Journal: "I Throw Rocks into the Water"

Twyckenham Notes: "New Orleans Botanical Garden"

Underwood Press: "One Moment"

My thanks also, to my mentor J. Marcus Weekley, with whose help this manuscript was completed.

For Jonathan

—the light in which these words were written

In remembrance

of Laura D'Arcangelo Norman & Mary Oliver

An owl sound wondered along the road with me.
I didn't hear it—I breathed it into my ears.

—William Stafford, "Malheur before Dawn"

We Americans are trained to think big, talk big, act big,
love big, admire bigness, but then the essential mystery
is in the small.

—Jim Harrison, *Off to the Side: A Memoir*

Contents

PART ONE

Bird City   1
You Know   2
Just as You Are   3
Daffodils   4
American Crow   6
I Throw Rocks into the Water   8
Another Moth   9
At Audubon Park, a Lady Asked   10
The Day Before My Youday, Marcus Writes—   11
Selected Poems of Carl Sandburg   12
As I Slept   13
Cat Benedictions   14
I Asked a Tibetan Monk to Help Renew Me. These are
    the Lines He Whispered One Morning, While His
    Frail Hand Covered My Eyes   15
Crossing Lake Pontchartrain, I Drive Through a Swarm
    of Blind Mosquitos   16
Li Po,   17
I Lie in Bed Late at Night in New Orleans   18
Falling Bridge   19
There's So Much Going On   20
The World Thinks the More You Know, the Closer You
    Get to God   21

Origami   22

A Poem Without Images   23

Semifaith   24

When Death Comes   25

Mary   26

Mother Bird   27

Who is My Father?   28

Why I Write About Birds   29

American Eye   30

Like a Ghost-bird at Night   32

Cascade   33

Yesterday I Cut the Grass   35

The Ant   36

On Becoming the Waves   37

Flock of the Future   38

Out in the Field   39

Rising Light   40

PART TWO

This Moment is Blue Jay   43

Louisiana Irises, Basking in the Sun   44

New Orleans Botanical Garden   45

Song of the Groundskeeper   46

Near the Mississippi, Early Morning   48

For What are the Blossoms Reaching?   49

Two Poems About Action   50

Drifting   51

Another Day in the Neighborhood   52

Some Days I Get So Frustrated   53

On Being Human   54

Trying to Save Her in the Twenty-First Century   55

To Baton Rouge on Our Anniversary   56

Hawk and Robin   57

On Visiting an Unnamed Swamp   58

Some Say the City is Louder   59

Where is My Mother?   60

The House Sparrow   61

On a Day Like Today, There's Nothing to be Excited About   62

Escaping the U.S.A.   63

To Always See the World as the Stray   65

I See the School Board Rush into the Café   66

New Orleans from the High-Rise Bridge   67

I Want to Rush Like the Fast-Moving Interstate   68

To Couturie Forest for a Drink   70

A Sand Poem I Wrote   71

Oily Gas Can   72

What More Could the Riverwalk Have Told Us?   73

At a Streetcar Stop   74

Three Miles: Two Children   75

Three Bedrooms, One Bath   76

One Moment   77

A Question About African Violets   78

Three Stories About Strangers   79

Somewhere, Duck   80

During Saga Dawa, I Walk to the Marsh; You Should
    Too   81

Notes   85

About   89

Part One

BIRD CITY

Walk to the top of Bird City tower, stare out—
feel weightless as a bee!

Oh, the burdens we carry—
like Nature carries night
where the car hits the fawn
crossing the road
for damp moonlit grass.

Burdens!—

they come quickly
like funnels,
rusty nails swirling,
shards of metal flinging
through the air like fangs
ripping arteries
in a stray dog fight.

Surely there's relief—
tranquility in the air!

Walk to the top of Bird City tower, stare out—

Even for a minute
you'll find the elegant army
of snowy egrets
diminish every burden—
with their stowed, bloodless swords—
like a thousand white peonies
soaring across the blue—

YOU KNOW

You know the way it goes—
you're sitting at work and a coworker comes to you,
or you are at the start of a reception,
or even a party (if you go to parties),

and while sipping a glass of Chardonnay,
or drinking a bottle of beer (if you drink beer),
a random person starts a conversation
that you might seem to enjoy at first,
until they take over the wheel

and veer you into the wall of a theater,
and start talking about a movie
they think is hilarious, with actors
you can't even pronounce, that they
assume you've watched a thousand times over.

And as we all have,
you stand stuck in the middle of a conversation
about a movie you've never seen
that you couldn't care less about—

cramped in a corner like a clueless ape,
you nod and laugh: "Ha ha!—Yep, yep!—I know!"

JUST AS YOU ARE

So the stork stands next to the man-made creek,

poking her needle-beak

down through thick grass,

as you might've gazed into the mirror this morning,
scrubbed your teeth,

stroked your hair, so does she
look through zoo-wire, stare at your face,

watching her own reflection blink
back.

DAFFODILS

Everything heals—everything—

even the doe, dead
next to the road. Hit
by a fast car late in the night,
when the driver,
who we'll never know, suddenly
saw her; slammed on brakes—her now limp body
flung to the ground.

Maybe she was thrown overboard a truck,
after a hunter, out seeking a trophy,
didn't have time to skin her for meat,
but shot her, anyway.

Now that time's passed,
she's no longer warm to our hand,
but to our heart, flaming—

what was a soon-to-be-mother,
one of four deer that stood in the distant field
every evening, nibbling winter-rye, lifting us
from what could be
a difficult world,

and so contently and peacefully flicked
the silk of her tail, next to the glimmering stream
at the hazy pink-flush
of sunrise.

Everything heals, I tell myself—*everything*—

***

Now, almost five months later,
passing the exact dip where she lay,
like a hand outstretched, offering the purest grace,
a group of yellow daffodils
here to save us.

AMERICAN CROW

on the side street
holding that acorn
in your mouth,

I wonder why you're
the symbol of death,
bad omen,
why not the white swan
or dove, why not
the cardinal or finch?

Why did you have to be
the last thing seen
before the shot rang out
at that house
on Bienville,
where we lived briefly,
three months,
and a man fell back-flat
right at our doorstep?

Are you Light
dressed in a different color,
and every wicked thing thought to be connected with you
is merely coincidence?

When I was a child
the best part
of my childhood
was when I ran far into the deep arms of the woods in morning
and heard your *caw*, your *caw,*

and down through the leggy pines,

perched peace, at the edge of my self,
thereafter.

I THROW ROCKS INTO THE WATER

What is it, gray and ridged,
sitting all to itself on a mound
of many others?

What is it now
that I recognize it, that I,
with my brief hand
choose it, pick it up, warm, and throw it in the water?

I watch it break
    the glass
        of the green lagoon.

Then a split silence

        it sinks:
        bubbles surface.

I throw another rock—
            shatter!

        Another—
            shatter!

And so close to nothing
        another long silence holds the air

as the last rock sinks farther
    and farther
        into the lagoon:

another still and untouched thing
    feels love.

ANOTHER MOTH

flies over the basket of clothes still warm from the dryer.

Oh well, her larvae
will infest this house.

Oh well, her larvae
will eat my clothes.

Oh well what others say

   —I let her live!

AT AUDUBON PARK, A LADY ASKED

"What's the name of those ducks
    on the water, the whistly ones

with orange bills?" The keeper,
    not really sure, said: "They fly here

from Brazil, eat our vegetation,
    shit on everything, then leave."

Like a dart aimed straight
    for the bull's-eye, on the first try—

the lady laughed—"Yeah!—
    A lot like humans!"

THE DAY BEFORE MY YOUDAY, MARCUS WRITES—

I've been reading through Anne's
All My Pretty Ones: I'd forgotten
how verbally facile she is! That girl
can write herself a phrase now! I'm amazed

Sylvia Plath gets so much airtime and Sexton
gets put in the kitchen with the cooks!

SELECTED POEMS OF CARL SANDBURG

Years before I was born
this book sat lost on its cage
of a shelf, watching and listening.

It heard sounds of the 1950s radio.
It heard the commotion when JF was killed.
It sat watching the first glint of Dorothy's red slippers when
the original Wizard of Oz aired in color.

Now, as I rub my hand over its page like a newfound puppy,
it lies with feet up, and tongue out
happily
having made it home.

AS I SLEPT

the glasses stood washed and lined
like perfect rows of corn
in the kitchen cabinet,
thankfully.

The towels were stowed
in their neat cubby, sleeping as I slept,
thankfully.

The tan blanket was perfectly draped
over the brown sofa,
thankfully.

After he arrived from work:
a glass was smudged dirty
with his lips and fingers,
thankfully.

His damp towel was thrown over the ironing board
with his musty socks,
thankfully.

The tan blanket was crumpled
like a wad on the floor,
thankfully.

CAT BENEDICTIONS

—One—

I could come home from work, pipes busted over the floor.
It would be like wading through a marshland with no damselfly,
no mottled duck, no mallow flower.

But I arrive at 6:06 p.m., the floor clean and dry, the cat
fast asleep in the window.

—Two—

When I wake, the cat could've pawed the liquid mulberry
potpourri at midnight, paw-prints trailed from one end of the
counter to the other. After licking the rich goodness from her
paw, sweet as honey, she could've been swole and sick.

But the alarm goes off, fresh coffee in the air. I step to the living
room: she's curled in a green pillow, purring, flicking the warm
of her ear.

I ASKED A TIBETAN MONK TO HELP RENEW ME. THESE ARE THE LINES HE WHISPERED ONE MORNING, WHILE HIS FRAIL HAND COVERED MY EYES

You've long desired
to climb Mt. Kailash,

to sit legs crossed
at the top, face up to clouds
that reach
down like warm hands,
like soft rain,
to wake you, to console
your pounding heart,

to make you
something you've never been,
the eye of the hummingbird—
a piece
of floating dust
on a dew droplet,
on a white
lotus blossom.

Listen,
he said,

become these crickets

chanting, chanting …

now, become the pale mist
you breathe in

out …

15

CROSSING LAKE PONTCHARTRAIN, I DRIVE THROUGH A SWARM OF BLIND MOSQUITOS

In the darks, out from the Causeway bridge, the lake makes moon-music for the sleeping moorhens deep within the reeds of the marshland. I hear nothing, only the rain of insects thumping the windshield, and a smell of fish oozing from those remains. Before they were rain, they saw a fast-moving light and rushed toward it. Now, I spray water over them and *swish* the wipers to clear my view. It is dark, and the drops of them sling from the blades at my moving sixty-five miles an hour. They flick— into the lake making moon-music, as far as I can see. They're glimmering, ripples of the moon, all around me.

LI PO,

I think of you and stay up late
into the night
and watch from my bedroom window,
the moon. I see it gleam on my pillow.
I hold my tea to its shining face
looking down on my shadow:

the reflection of who I was

                    leaving the room behind me.

I LIE IN BED
LATE AT NIGHT
IN NEW ORLEANS

I hear cars honk
    like three brothers arguing
        near an open window.

The youngest squeals off—
    then into the distance
        —*vroom* the others …

FALLING BRIDGE

While you drive over the rusty bridge, loud with clicks and pops,
    cracks crawling
the piers: it crumbles, splats into water (luckily
you're safe); this doesn't mean that just you caused the

                                                    c
                                              r
                                          u
                                              m
                                                b
                                                  l
                                                    i
                                                      n
                                                          g
                                      d
                                        o
                                            w
                                              n
                                                  .

What about the lack of maintenance from the city? What
about the community? What
about rain, heat, ice, over the years,
wearing it
                 d
                   o
                      w
                         n
                s
                 l
                    o
                      w
                        l
                          y
                           ,
    g
      r
       a
         d
          u
            a
              l
                l
              y
               ?

THERE'S SO MUCH GOING ON

trash is thrown from windows,
   others pick it up, fathers
argue on their phones, many
   end with *love you,*
cars *vroom* up the inter-
   state, some squeal

to slow down. Joined
   to this world, is another
we mustn't forget,
   which is undoubtedly, the
same world: the *whoosh*
   of waves onto the shore,

the split second thereafter,
   Mockingbird's call at
sunrise, her absence
   by afternoon, the quietest
lull in evening—then through
   air: cicadas ringing!

THE WORLD THINKS THE MORE YOU KNOW, THE CLOSER YOU GET TO GOD

Think of this: knowledge knows how to fix the washer when it stops. It can reach Moon. It knows precisely how the fleshly mechanics of Hummingbird, reach down into the deep cup of Red Trumpet, and drink, drink, drink. Not knowing is just as powerful. Sit on a bench in City Park and think about Swan, what she might ponder as she glides over that movable glass. Think of the wonders that could find us—Mockingbird, Warbler, Sparrow—a free ticket to the art museum. If you're a gambler perhaps, you could win the lottery of surprise, when Egret and Heron rise from the lake to address you by name. Marvel in possibilities! Love imagination! What would happen to this, if you knew?

ORIGAMI

Bob Dylan, said,

"He not busy being born is busy dying."
    This is why I sit on the floor and make
        origami, with J., something I've
never made before, only seen at museums
in folds of color.

    "He not busy being born is busy dying."
    This is why I make tea different this
    morning: add honey, less leaves to taste the
    soft sweet delicacy of earth, the way the
    green-backed tit alights on a branch in early
    morning China.

    "He not busy being born is busy dying."
This is why deep inside, I fold in, out, like the wing
    of the paper swan—why I pop open
from the glum flat womb of the wretched
    past, into the glorious day, of this first light!

A POEM WITHOUT IMAGES

Nothing.

Nothing, nothing.

Nothing; nothing; nothing

—Nothing.

SEMIFAITH

Even though the lights went out,
I hear the barred owl, the frogs'
ribbiting across the river.

I sit on these steps, smell the
organic earth, all that once was,
now the sweet scent of earth.

Though the lights are out, I brush
the tender tops of tulips, wet,
with evening dew.

I stroll through the night, sure and
hopeful, having never laid eyes
on Spring.

WHEN DEATH COMES

I remove my shovel from the soil.
I switch off the mower's engine.

I remove my boots and prop my feet above the ground.

I do not get in my way. I do not hesitate.
I whisper, *Everything's so alive, let me not disturb it.*

I lie down in the vacuum of my ash, for what must be an eternity—
I become the becoming

MARY

—in response to Mary Oliver's "I'm Not the River"

Now, I am the river
that roiling presence.
I'm the black oak tree—
patience personified.
I am redbird
a brief life heartily enjoyed.
Now I'm mud and rock and sand
holding everything together.
Now, I am all of these things, yes always.

MOTHER BIRD

When despair comes a sudden weight
and all you think is death—

remember mother bird's
beak-of-seeds

shoved
down
baby-
bird's
neck.

WHO IS MY FATHER?

You?

You?

YO!

WHY I WRITE ABOUT BIRDS

Birds are so much like the gays:
gays at a straight cousin's funeral,
gays in line for a chicken sandwich,
    gays trying to find a comfortable room
      on vacation.

They say that birds do not
belong here (behind the walls
of a poem); they say they're too small,
    trite; and they want them *out,   Out*—

                              OUT!

AMERICAN EYE

O starling jet fighter
come to see me
this 22nd of February,
traveled from Eurasia,
seen as foreign,
as invasive as the finch.
You stunning
as the American birds
perched on the fence
with your miraculous
black beak of winter,
tipped in yellow
that will soon
cover the whole in
spring. How miraculous
your beak changes
color, that in the
19th century
you sailed across the
Atlantic, that now, you
look at me with your
deep right eye as I feed
chickens in this urban
yard. You, one-
legged amazement
of speckled iridescent
green, limping on the
feeder, O, beautiful
as the native birds,
oblivious of your hapless past:

spread your wings—
become yourself, you,
native to my American eye
as all the others.

LIKE A GHOST-BIRD AT NIGHT

I soar through our old neighborhood
above the worn-out road. I see where we planted
two magnolia trees in the front yard, walked
the dogs, the road sign still the same.

I don't recognize faces. Some on the porch in their rockers,
others behind closed doors with nothing to discern but the flicker
of the television. If this were really me, I'd think I'd woken from a deep sleep
in someone else's home.

But neither of us are there,
not even our memory.

CASCADE

Everything on earth has blossom:
a pale pink
or purple passionflower
gives life to the hummingbird
or bee—
      or as the bee
         to the fuchsia—
      or as the fuchsia
         to the seed.

Even wolves in their bloodstained fur
      give life:
         snarling,
         running necks and ribs,
         tearing and pulling,
         ripping down—
yet out of the wolves
come blossom.

How can such viciousness bring virtue?

      When vegetation vanishes
   within the stomach
of elk
or whitetail—
      when the forest floor
is as flat as war—

Then out
of the wolves' kill
                sprout aspen …

emerge beavers, and
cottonwoods,
                shrikes soar!

YESTERDAY I CUT THE GRASS

Yesterday   I cut the grass,
     and today
          I see short
              tender sprigs
soaring   their way back
up bright   and joyful!

O hundreds
     and hundreds of sprigs,
when   the world cuts me up—
spits me out—please—
let me be
        as buoyant—

        as forgiving!

THE ANT

You can't help the life you were given, like the ant can't help hers,

the one crawling the white wall at work, in the bathroom, where

my hands, tied to the clock, can't help, and where there are no windows.

I shut the door behind me, think, how will she survive?

Through the smallest crevice somewhere, I know she will.

ON BECOMING THE WAVES

Somewhere the waves are alive. Like an endless longing they pull from the vast body of blue, and push forward to the sanderling—white and brown—who when the waves come, scurries away, then back to the receding water to eat from the foamy sand.

What does it mean that waves are relentless—that no matter where, no matter what they're going through, they pull, and push?

Close your eyes and think of terns. In your darkest hour imagine gulls lifting intermingled from the shore. Beyond them, become the waves rising, knowing the worst can never stop you—reach, reach again: that glimmering shore!

FLOCK OF THE FUTURE

I see six of them, far away, rise into the air like sudden gifts. They float above traffic, as white as I can see, which makes me wonder what it'd be like if suddenly, every bird became extinct.

What would it be like then, not having their wing and song, not having their wonder; certainly we all in this heavy world need it.

I drive closer and closer. I am taken aback by their thin plastic wings, how they are grocery bags drifting, snagging through traffic—and—like some foreign exchange of birds, rise back up again …

OUT IN THE FIELD

With his lone pen he runs like a dog through clover, lips rising and
falling.

He snaps at thoughts that dart into the space in front of him.

Once the flock rises high and far—he shuts his notebook, grabs his
pen, lifts his cup of coffee,

and like a panting dog tired with mud and grit, hits the sidewalk,
for his long journey, home.

RISING LIGHT

—for Jonathan

I don't know how to tell you
  how it feels to be loved

until this morning I got up,
  made the bed, walked
    to the Zen-room from where

a light was shining.
  He was sitting in the desk-chair
    like a flowing river typing a report.
      He stood and we put our arms
      around each other.

Like hearing the trickle of water
  from an early morning
    riverbank, I felt the release
    of my every muscle,
      my every bone giving way—
      to the rising light.

Part Two

THIS MOMENT IS BLUE JAY

jeering and jeering—
       (this you, this me, this spicebush swallowtail
          bowing in the muddy soil at the edge
    of the green lagoon)

It jeers through the trees—
     this moment never uttered before—
     this one-of-a-kind

     gift, now perched, now vivid blue, now
        wing-up over the green leaving—

     us the sound of leaves rustling …

LOUISIANA IRISES, BASKING IN THE SUN

These
purple
mouths
bright
as flame,

hold out
their
tongues

for drops

of rain.

NEW ORLEANS BOTANICAL GARDEN

Everyone's admiring the Fiddle-leaf Plumeria;
    the Bougainvillea, waving its body of pink leaves;
        the blue Morning Glories,
            gripped to the trellis.

Everyone's admiring the Victoria Water Lilly,
    holding its white star; the large Staghorn Fern;
        the Dancing Girl Ginger.

And what's most admirable, is all the admiring:
    each person leaned into a plant, whispering
        behind their eyes—
            I love you. I love you.

SONG OF THE GROUNDSKEEPER

You can keep
the highest
paying job,
she said.

You can keep
all the stress
and politics.

You can keep
the fancy
building
down the block.

But please,
please let
me keep
this yard
with Squirrel,
with Jasmine.

Let me keep
this lawn
with Oak
and Dragonfly.

I'd much rather
have the leftovers,
like this walk
picking up trash,

me laughing
internally
at White Ibis,
silly looking,
picking around
the grass—

NEAR THE MISSISSIPPI, EARLY MORNING

A platoon of a dozen soldiers stomps
boots at the dusk of dawn, preparing for war.

Behind me: a flock of a thousand whistler ducks—black-bellied—
whistle and whistle through the trees—

What if they vanish—leave a world of machinery and war?

I think about the soldiers marching, as if they're waning off
the face of Earth.

Where might we be, or not be, without them?

Pelicans go sailing low and hard.
I listen to the ducks—whistling and whistling;
the soldiers marching, marching, in the distance …

FOR WHAT ARE THE BLOSSOMS REACHING?

As you too might wonder, I wonder who is God.

    Does She have a name, does He not? Is It a thing

like the penny or bottle cap? Do They exist

    like the llama or quail?

I lie, back-flat to summer grass. A canopy

    of branches above me, each thick

with brilliant leaves and fragrant magnolia blossoms—

    reaching their awake petal-arms

for that warm, mysterious *light*, from the sun.

TWO POEMS ABOUT ACTION

—One—

Try reading about something that isn't moving. The green chair for instance. Over there. Still. By itself. Doing nothing. Sitting. Sitting.

—Two—

Now try reading about the man running down Murat, in pink cowboy boots, cutoffs, long beard, crack showing bent over chasing a piece of paper, gritting teeth, tripping through stop sign, red corvette slamming on breaks, laying on horn, holding up middle finger; and Blue Jay soaring past it all, at tail end of it, paper finally in hand, red corvette taillights far up ahead. High trees shed the colors of Fall.

DRIFTING

This morning I sat in the backyard
  and a froghopper crawled over my
    hand, and at the crevasse of my
      thumb, jumped out her wings, and drifted away—

  Late yesterday, the river forced forward—
    all the way to the Gulf. The muddy water
      before my eyes no longer the same, drifted away—

    Two months ago, we watched elk in Cherokee
      graze over a field, the birds paused
        in their melodious note. Like leaves rolling
          into dusk, we slipped in our car, and drifted: today—

ANOTHER DAY IN THE NEIGHBORHOOD

Our neighbors never complain about our chickens;
instead, they let sparrows sing at their feeder,
let trees shutter and never pollute the air with noise.

Early one morning distraught rang wall to wall,
from ceiling to ceiling. We were in bed and heard from their house:
"HOW COULD YOU, CHRIS! HOW COULD YOU!"

We think he found happiness with another woman, or perhaps a man;
and there, like ripping back a sheet, she caught him.

It's been three weeks and we're all still upset with Chris:
his ex for walking in on him at one in the morning;
us in the thick air of new neighbors:
grinding saws, throwing parties, their kids squealing
everywhere ...

SOME DAYS I GET SO FRUSTRATED

NO DEEK, don't get on the couch!
DOVA, don't bark at your brother!
DICHTER, don't eat your sister's food!

And like the moth fluttering past my ear—
I'm reminded
of how short
their life is,
of what a miracle
their life is,
so my whole demeanor
begins:

Here Deek, have this potato chip!
Dova, roll around as much as you want
on the new rug!

Here, let me rub your belly
and between your ears,
as you lay your head on my chest,

and dream, what only dogs dream …

ON BEING HUMAN

—thank you, Ashley

You get an instruction manual
    for everything:
the little fish tank you put together
    last summer, with the fancy filter;
the record player you bought as a surprise;
the vacuum cleaner; the lawn mower;
    the trampoline. I'm sure, stuffed away,
you have a cabinet filled with them:
those little fan-papers of writing dry as sand.
Even the cheap toaster you bought from Walmart
    has one, as does the blender,
the fancy birdfeeder,
the one with gadgets to keep away the squirrels.

But for the most complicated of machines,
    the most complex of systems,
what do we get? No manual,
no lessons on how to use it: only a burst—
of sudden light, a trillion circumstances,
and somewhere within
a hundred years to figure it out.

TRYING TO SAVE HER IN THE TWENTY-FIRST CENTURY

It's five a.m.
and the refrigerator barks
like a baby seal
that lost its mother.

Somewhere in a Louisiana swamp
the same thing is happening—
a nest of blue heron chicks cheep
and cheep—
yet silence and wind dance together
a solemn dance.

It's happening all across America,
and in Asia, and Mexico,
and it doesn't stop there. Whales
off the coast of Africa
are panicking too,
and so are elephants
and wolves running franticly through the fields.

Brothers and sisters
and their kids too—
so am I, so are all of us,
trying to save Mother ...

TO BATON ROUGE ON OUR ANNIVERSARY

We flap along the interstate:
suddenly, like a log across our view,
it's Alligator,
with bowed legs, chin forward
for the other side.

We swerve hard
to the left, miss, and panic
looking in the rearview mirror
for what other machines rush ahead—

In this South, I expect large
trucks to see vulnerable creatures
as opportunities—
to smash with pride and boast:
"I'm a man!"
But the big-wheeled truck
with winch,
swerves, and *vrooms* forward—

My Cynic says: they were trying to save
the underside of their vehicle.

My Hopeful says: they didn't want to see blood-guts
        sprayed over the street—
another dead animal fly-ridden,
rolled over week
after week.

HAWK AND ROBIN

I am the hawk flying over River Road,
next to the Mississippi, and you are the robin
clenched by my claw, and now I am the robin,
just as you are.

I am the hawk, just as you are, and together
we eat the earth, and become the earth,
and on we go being eaten by the earth.

You are the robin, just as I am. I am the
hawk flying over River Road, next to the
Mississippi, with a robin clenched in my claw,
and so are you.

ON VISITING AN UNNAMED
SWAMP

Amid high brown cypress in thick
dark air, amid the scent of dirt

and fern, Water Moccasin
lurks head-up, through

black water—question mark,
after question mark.

Cicadas in the distance—
whine, whine. Some-

where between they entwine
with crickets' chirp

lacing through the dark air—
O what throbs, and throbs, of faint light.

SOME SAY THE CITY IS LOUDER

that it speaks of many, many things.
But I ask:

if you stand in the middle,
what do you hear? The sound of a trolley,
an ambulance, a frustrated driver
behind a braked car?

A bell?   A yell?   A plane?

What if you escape—
sail miles and miles, sit under
a blue moon at the edge of midnight—
waves crashing on the shore?

What is louder then, the vast city,
the starry ocean?

What about silence

                    between the waves?

WHERE IS MY MOTHER?

my mother …

other

THE HOUSE SPARROW

with
the
black
bib

flits
to
the
perch
of
the
hanging
feeder.

From
his
stout
beak
seeds
crumble
to
the
ground

,

and
with
a flash-
jerk—

he's
gone !

ON A DAY LIKE TODAY, THERE'S NOTHING TO BE EXCITED ABOUT

Not a bird ferrying light into the yard,
not a noisy neighbor, clanking pots, preparing crawfish to boil.
It's early spring and all the blossoms are folded
asleep in their buds, snoozing—

Off to my right above the plucked brown sludge
from where I moved the chicken coop,
I see a fist of what must be, a hundred juicy flies, swarming.

It's not the sweet half-eaten melon
that's thrilling them, or a sugary drink tipped
over the ground; instead, it's a muck
of flattened chicken manure.

Today, when there's only the reek of where the chicken coop
used to be, and a fist of elated flies,
I'm proven wrong—yes!—
there's something to be excited about!

ESCAPING THE U.S.A.

I sit here in this popping café.
Politics swing fits around me.
I read a book, glance up
every once in a while, look
back at the book, then up at fans
twirling like helicopters refusing to land.

I think of monarchs I saw
this morning at the edge of Big Lake,
orange with black paisley filling their wings,
how they wove around me
and straight through the passersby,
fluttering through traffic to the other side.

I wonder:
  do they know getting across—
  is a miracle?

I'm here, at what seems
like the other side of that world,
in a dimly lit building drinking mocha
in the middle of afternoon, walls
and concrete surround me.
The horrible quarrels
of a country I want to escape.

I long
to be as close as possible to the pure earth,
the tender leaves,
the thick open arms of the oaks.

But I sit watching these fans spin round
and round in this conflicted country.

I drift, as I usually do
in settings like this,
so far that I begin to think
of the built world
and natural world
as the one world that it is:
dragonflies swarm and pick me up
with their millions of wings;
the fans tear
from the ceiling like seeds of maples
spinning propellers
through the sky. All of us rise and break free
with a zeal like the monarchs migrating
south,

down deep across the warm gulf,

into the neovolcanic belt
of that dear sweet country,

Mexico.

TO ALWAYS SEE THE WORLD AS THE STRAY

The world is not broke, but mending; each day there's not only death, there's hope. You've heard it—the boy saved from the alligator? What about the girl with the prosthetic leg, no longer locked to the bed? Why does the world have to fall apart; why does it have to be ending? Spring is here, Robin has laid her eggs, dandelions sprout everywhere! I hope to always see the world as the stray running our neighborhood: she never thinks about the meals she's missed—only notices the pan of hearty ones she's given.

I SEE THE SCHOOL BOARD
RUSH INTO THE CAFÉ

They're stunning
    in black
        and white suits, like terns

off the shore of Aruba, soaring
    in to work, typing a bit,
        drinking a glass

of lemon water, only.
    They clap
        their computers

after 10 minutes:
    push them
        into their bags, flee

the table, leave only a feather
    of paper. Once here,
        now gone, they soar—

into the world—
        making it beautiful!
        —I'm hopeful—
        and more beautiful!

NEW ORLEANS FROM THE HIGH-RISE BRIDGE

At night
atop the High-Rise
her buildings house
a thousand gleaming
fireflies, signaling—

During the day
she's another thing
we pass: a lousy
light pole, a rusty fire hydrant
an untamed tennis court.

Here,
here!
I'm the place to be!
I'm the place to see!
I'm Jazzy!

I WANT TO RUSH LIKE THE FAST-MOVING INTERSTATE

to City Park,
watch gulls
swoop
for tossed bread,
wander the edge
of Bayou St. John
where miraculous
people cluster
like mixed phlox
in spring, around
smoking grills
and sprawled
blankets.

I want
to watch dogs
run up
and down
the bayou, tongues
dangling happily
from side
to side, but

I'm sitting
in this yard
with a book
absorbing
now—like a simple
meditation—
reading tiny
redbugs

as if words
from God,
crawling across like sentences on the white page.

TO COUTURIE FOREST FOR A DRINK

This fall is a rare one. I teach a morning class only, get off at 11:50 a.m., and have the rest of the day for myself. What a scarce thing to have in today's world, time, so when they asked me to stay after for a six-hour meeting, about a new online platform, I ran to every excuse under the sun, like a man dehydrated, scurrying everywhere for water. Soon after, I slid in my car and drove to the forest, skipped through oaks and pines, twirled my body, flapped my arms like blue bills splashing the water.

I wonder what would've happened had I stayed for that meeting, had I sat those six miserable hours in that sterile white room meant to rob me of Cricket, of Bluebird, of Wood Duck. What would've happened, or might not have happened, had I missed the vee of geese exclaiming overhead, if like some dehydrated maniac of a man, I'd continued living without water?

A SAND POEM I WROTE

—————Next to the River

OILY GAS CAN

Needing to rid it of old gas and fill it with new,
I carry it to a hole in the yard and let it gush
and fume over the mud.

How hundreds jump from a building-fire—
or dive out of a sinking ship—
how a fresh wound feels when opened and poured with salt—
a certain number of earthworms plunge from the muck
and *squirm.*

I'll never know if they lived
(I couldn't stick around to watch).

I'll never do that again.

WHAT MORE COULD THE RIVERWALK HAVE TOLD US?

Yesterday, J. and I went where locals never go,
to the Riverwalk, and ate something
we never eat, Mona's Lebanese.

Instead of sitting inside the mall
we sat outside.

Seagulls begged and laughed, circled overhead.

If I were a cynic, I'd say they'd shit
in our food, but we took the risk,
and took it in.

Beneath us was a little house sparrow
chunky as a bee, with all days' meal
a little greasy under its neck.

It hopped around and looked at us
with its little eye, as if to ask,
where is mine?

The Mississippi forced forward—
never looking back.

We raised our forks of grape leaves
to tzatziki.

What more could the Riverwalk have told us—

Is this what it means to live?

AT A STREETCAR STOP

Two old men argue
about last night's game;
I smell diesel and oil.

A young man sits
next to me, with his wife
and young boy, then flicks
a half-smoked cigarette
to the sand at our feet.

I look at the back of my lids
and imagine this spot
hundreds of years ago:
lush and tall with pines,
green and thriving.

When I open them
a stream of cigarette smoke floats
above our feet
and a Snickers wrapper—

time burning and burning
amid two pink barrettes
and a Solo cup.

THREE MILES: TWO CHILDREN

I pass rich white houses
and there—
bundled in three layers of clothes,
holding mommy's hand
and a Toy Story lunchbox—
a boy
skips his way to school.

Then passing the 9th Ward
another child—
roaming in rags, barefoot, skinny—
finds her way alone
back
to the city …

THREE BEDROOMS, ONE BATH

—First Room—

I hear J's phone laughing out a video in the
bedroom. I sit in the living room reading a
book: "SHUT THE DOOR!"

—Second Room—

The pups scratch and playful growl. "Nah-eah!"
I say, and shut the door.

—Third Room—

The bird, happy to be warm in our house,
sputters out a new song—
I cover his cage, shut the door.

***

—Bath—

How foolish of me to shut them out—
those, love me most.

ONE MOMENT

A cardinal flits around the myrtle tree, tweets into the yellow rise of morning, and my dog, Deek, hops around the yard like a slow hare, out of a burrow in spring. He eats grass for what must be an upset stomach. The cardinal tweets and tweets. Then like a toilet plunger sucking a thick clog, Deek heaves and heaves, then gags it up, while the cardinal tweets from a different branch now. What relief he must feel—walking to lap up water from a partly rusted pail. And the cardinal tweets and tweets and tweets ...

A QUESTION
ABOUT AFRICAN VIOLETS

—thank you, Christine

At a woman's house
  of gloom,
    and misery,
   and despair,
and misfortune,

in her back room
  under small
    fluorescent lamps—
   hundreds
  of African Violets!—
 vibrant
and stunning!

In your house
  of gloom,
    and difficulty,
   and blue funk,
and dismay—

  where do yours
   bloom?

THREE STORIES ABOUT STRANGERS

—One—

Noreen, our waitress at the African restaurant, who we'd never met, sat with J. and me like old friends, told stories about her past, about her little Pontiac Firebird of a car, how it picked-up, zoomed, how the police once chased her on her way through Florida. At the end she filled our tea for the last time, took our money, gave us each a fist bump and spirit fingers, then turned away. We haven't seen her since.

—Two—

Last week at Olive Garden, a young man on a first date choked on what must've been a cherry tomato. A starched older man, eating dinner with his wife from the flipside of the booth, sprang up and did the Heimlich. Once his throat was clear, the young man gave the older man a quick, full hug. Both sat and ate the rest of their dinner, backs to one another. When finished each walked their separate way, driving far on opposite roads, home.

—Three—

Pushing a cart through Sam's, I stopped to study the black grapes and moseyed to the red ones. Holding a pack in hand, a man nudged me "These any good?" "I normally get the black ones, over there," I said, "but they're too soft." "Yeah, I don't like soft grapes either," and with a pack of red ones in hand, he eased back to his husband's cart, and they went on, shopping.

SOMEWHERE, DUCK

It's true that somewhere, Duck lives her life casually on the water: maybe eating a few bugs and roots, maybe a few boys throw sticks at her; maybe she's small enough to rise into the air over the pond and buildings.

Most days the weight and worry of the world pull me down. It's then that I think about Duck, how she faces her day with grace and weightlessness, how no matter what happens she claps her bill and makes a way.

How everything in the world is a part of everything else. How I am the green water, calm, happy. I am Duck eating this tear of bread, from my hand.

DURING SAGA DAWA, I WALK TO THE MARSH; YOU SHOULD TOO

Get there early on a day of spotty rain;
be on the muddy path and find
contentment with damp clothes.

You'll hear palmettos off to the side,
yaupons on your way. You'll hear
shuffling under leaves, feel the sharp sting
hit your skin, though you're covered
in bug spray.

You'll walk in the dark and ever more darkness
of the wood, until there is light
at the end of the tunnel-leaves, streaks
from under a field of water hyacinth and duckweed.

You'll think you can tiptoe over them,
and you will want to
when you see far over sky-patches of water,
mangrove green—

Great Egret moving in sleek motion,
moorhens like shadows
scooting across your view.

You'll hear beyond your shoulder
through the pink flush of sky—
the *conk-a-reee!* of the red-winged blackbird amid cordgrass
and cattails.

Inhaling the sugared earth, you'll want to die
with the songs of the amphibial trillions.
You'll want to die.

You'll want to die and live it over
and over again,

   as they do

NOTES

"American Eye"

The European starling is native to Eurasia. It is said that these birds were introduced to North America in the late 1890s by Eugene Schieffelin, out of hope that all birds mentioned in the literature of Shakespeare would become established in the New World. Today, the European starling is widely considered an invasive species in North America and is grudgingly admired by the National Audubon Society for its adaptability, toughness, and intelligence.

"Bird City"

In the 1890s when plume hunters hunted snowy egrets to near extinction, Edward Avery McIlhenny raised and released eight young egrets on his Louisiana property in the fall of 1895 to migrate across the Gulf of Mexico; to his surprise six of the birds returned to nest in spring. In 1911, sixteen years after the release, McIlhenny estimated that one hundred thousand birds were nesting at what is now known as Bird City, a private bird sanctuary located on Avery Island in Iberia Parish, Louisiana.

"Crossing Lake Pontchartrain, I Drive Through a Swarm of Blind Mosquitos"

Aquatic midges, commonly known as blind mosquitos, are an insect found around lakes, rivers, and artificial water systems. These insects are not blind, do not bite, and can swarm in the billions. Due to polluted Mississippi River waters released into Lake Pontchartrain, these insects have begun to multiply rapidly there. Blind mosquitos are an important food source for fish, and their larvae clean aquatic environments by filtering pollutants from the water.

"During Saga Dawa, I Walk to the Marsh; You Should Too"

Saga Dawa is one of the most sacred holidays in the Tibetan Buddhism tradition, taking place during the fourth month of the Tibetan lunar calendar, usually beginning in May and ending in June on the Gregorian calendar. This holiday month is all about making merit and peaks on full moon day, Saga Dawa Duchen. Those who practice Tibetan Buddhism usually refrain from eating meat, give money to the less fortunate, and make pilgrimages to holy places during this time.

"Mary"

Writing "Mary" in response to Mary Oliver's poem "I'm Not the River," from her book *Blue Horses*, gave me closure with her death. While writing this poem, I stayed as close as possible to Mary's original voice, only removing and replacing keywords and punctuation to guide her voice to tell, what I imagine it longs to tell, that she's no longer with us in human flesh form.

"Origami"

The quote "He not busy being born is busy dying" comes from Bob Dylan's song "It's Alright, Ma" released in 1965. Dylan used this song—which acknowledges that we Americans are always being fed a false reality—to vent about commercialism, consumerism, and war mentality in contemporary America. Hearing it one day, or reading it somewhere, set fireflies off in my head and inspired me.

"Proem," a term used in the subtitle of this collection, is a third genre which falls between verse and prose. It's a more open term than "prose poem" or "flash fiction," where the terms, through their names, lean more toward verse or prose. "Proem" does not favor one over the other, and therefore encompasses prose poems, flash fictions, and those works that fall in-between.

My mentor, J. Marcus Weekley, first introduced me to the term back in 2018, and I've been using it ever since. Thank you, Marcus!

The name "Deek," which appears in "Some Days I Get So Frustrated" and "One Moment," is my dog Dichter's nickname.

—A.

ABOUT

Ahrend Torrey earned his MA/MFA in creative writing from Wilkes University in Wilkes-Barre, Pennsylvania, and is the author of *Small Blue Harbor*, published by the Poetry Box Select imprint in 2019. His work has appeared in *The Greensboro Review*, *The Perch* (a journal of the Yale Program for Recovery and Community Health, a program of the Yale School of Medicine) and *West Trade Review*, among others. He is also a recipient of the Etruscan Prize awarded by Etruscan Press. He lives in southern Louisiana with his husband Jonathan, and is working on several new collections of poetry.

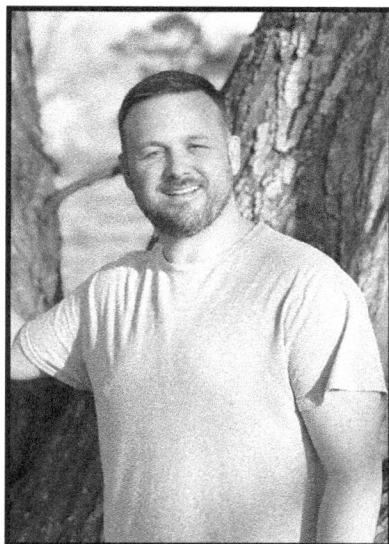

www.ingramcontent.com/pod-product-compliance
Lightning Source LLC
Chambersburg PA
CBHW030958090426
42737CB00007B/591